W9-AVM-353

First Facts®

American Indian Homes

PUEBLOS

by Jack Manning

CAPSTONE PRESS
a capstone imprint

First Facts are published by Capstone Press,
1710 Roe Crest Drive, North Mankato, Minnesota 56003
www.capstonepub.com

Library of Congress Cataloging-in-Publication Data
Manning, Jack.
 Pueblos / by Jack Manning.
   pages cm. – (First facts. American Indian homes)
 Includes bibliographical references and index.
 Summary: "Informative, engaging text and vivid photos introduce readers to pueblos"—Provided by publisher.
  ISBN 978-1-4914-0315-0 (library binding)
  ISBN 978-1-4914-0319-8 (paperback)
  ISBN 978-1-4914-0323-5 (eBook PDF)

  33614080655359

 1. Pueblos—Juvenile literature. 2. Pueblo Indians—Juvenile literature. 3. Pueblo architecture—Juvenile literature. I. Title.
 E99.P9M32 2015
 978.9004'974—dc23

            2014008073

Editorial Credits
Brenda Haugen, editor; Kyle Grenz, designer; Jo Miller, media researcher;
Kathy McColley, production specialist

Photo Credits
123RF: Jerry Rainey, 11; Alamy: David South, 5, North Wind Picture Archives, 9; Cartesia, 6 (map); Corbis, 17; Newscom: akg-images, 15; Shutterstock: Gary Saxe, 3, mark higgins, 7, Pecold, cover, qingqing, 13, Sumikophoto, 19, 21, Terry W Ryder, 1

Design Elements
Shutterstock: Crystal Eye Studio, elnavegante, quingqing

Printed in the United States of America in North Mankato, Minnesota.
032014   008087CGF14

Table of Contents

What Is a Pueblo?

Pueblos are houses built with **adobe** bricks or **sandstone**. American Indians in the southwestern United States built these houses hundreds of years ago.

In the mid-1500s, Spanish **explorers** came to the Southwest. They used the word pueblo to describe the houses and the people who lived in them.

---

adobe—a building material made of clay mixed with straw and dried in the sun

sandstone—rock that includes sand and some cement

explorer—a person who goes to an unknown place

---

a pueblo in New Mexico

FACT

Many of the American Indians who lived in pueblos were farmers. They grew corn and other crops.

Chapter 2

Who Lived in Pueblos?

The **ancestors** of the Pueblo Indians first lived in pueblos. They are often called the Anasazi. They carved pueblos into the sandstone walls of **cliffs**.

The first pueblo builders are the ancestors of many **tribes** of Pueblo Indians. Each of these tribes built pueblos. Some American Indians still live in pueblos.

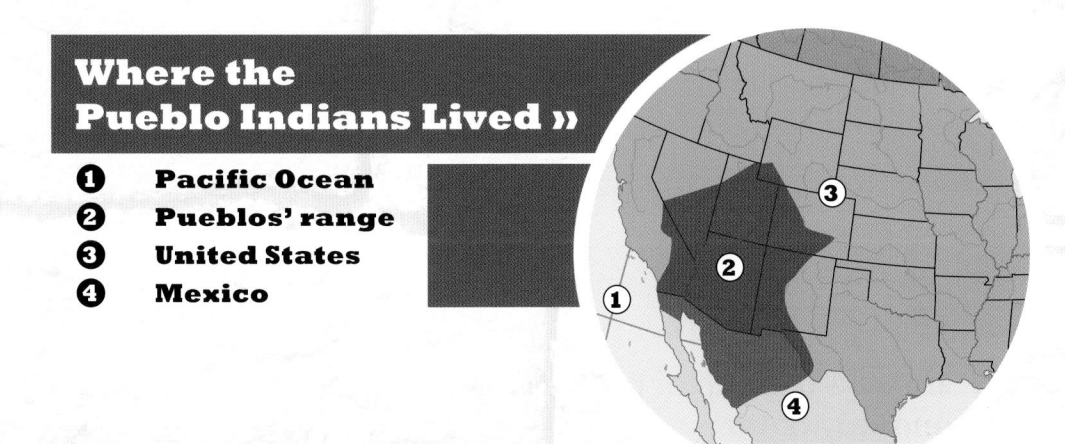

Where the Pueblo Indians Lived »

1. Pacific Ocean
2. Pueblos' range
3. United States
4. Mexico

ancestor—a family member who lived a long time ago

cliff—a high, steep rock face

tribe—a group of people who share the same language and way of life

Gathering Materials

The Pueblo Indians used materials found in nature to build their houses. People carved sandstone from cliffs. People dug the clay from riverbanks to make bricks.

Men searched for wood to use for the roofs of their homes. Wood was hard to find in many parts of the Southwest. The men traveled to the mountains to cut trees for wood.

People found materials near rivers to build pueblos.

Chapter 4

Preparing the Materials

Builders made blocks or bricks for their pueblos. Some builders used stone tools to carve and shape sandstone into smooth blocks. Others made adobe bricks with clay, water, and straw. They shaped the mixture into bricks and dried them in the sun.

FACT

Before work began on a pueblo, a village chief would say a prayer. The chief prayed to keep the family and home safe.

A mixture of clay, water, and straw is formed into bricks.

Building a Pueblo

People first built a pueblo's walls. Builders stacked rows of sandstone blocks or adobe bricks to build the walls. Mud held the blocks or bricks in place.

After the walls were finished, builders added a roof. The roof was made from logs and smaller pieces of wood. They covered the roof and walls with wet clay.

FACT

Many pueblos had three or four levels. The rooms were built on top of one another.

Inside a Pueblo

Pueblos were simple homes. A fireplace warmed the house at night. Several built-in shelves stored supplies.

The Pueblo Indians made good use of small spaces. People sometimes hung a pole from the ceiling. They used the pole as a clothes rack. Rooftops were used for cooking and other **chores**.

chore—a job that has to be done regularly; washing dishes and taking out the garbage are chores

A family gathers in their pueblo.

Early pueblos did not have doors. People used a ladder to climb in and out through a hole in the roof.

Chapter 7

Pueblo Villages

A pueblo village had many homes that were built close together. The Pueblo Indians built their homes around a square. They used the center square area for games and special events.

Women owned the family pueblo. Each family lived in one large room. As a family grew, they added more rooms and levels.

Pueblo Indians hold a special dance in the village square.

Chapter 8

Special Rooms

Each village had an underground room called a **kiva**. It was used for **ceremonies** and meetings.

The Pueblo Indians believed they came from a world below the earth. They thought the kiva linked their ceremonies to the other world. They believed the ladder down into a kiva joined the two worlds together.

---

kiva—an underground room used for ceremonies and meetings

ceremony—formal actions, words, and often music performed to mark an important occasion

---

People used a ladder to climb down into a kiva.

Pueblos Today

Pueblos are still part of the southwestern United States. People can tour Anasazi **ruins** at national parks. Visitors to New Mexico also can find pueblos where people still live.

Amazing but True

Can you imagine a city made of gold? In the 1500s pueblos were wrongly thought to be made of gold. In 1540 Spanish explorer Francisco Vasquez de Coronado was looking for the Seven Cities of Gold. He actually found villages belonging to a Pueblo tribe. The villages only looked golden from a distance.

pueblos at Mesa Verde National Park in Colorado

ruins—the remains of something that has collapsed or been destroyed

Glossary

adobe (uh-DOH-bee)—a building material made of clay mixed with straw and dried in the sun

ancestor (AN-sess-tuhr)—a family member who lived a long time ago

ceremony (SER-uh-moh-nee)—formal actions, words, and often music performed to mark an important occasion

chore (CHOR)—a job that has to be done regularly; washing dishes and taking out the garbage are chores

cliff (KLIF)—a high, steep rock face

explorer (ik-SPLOR-ur)—a person who goes to an unknown place

kiva (KEE-vah)—an underground room used for ceremonies and meetings

ruins (ROO-ins)—the remains of something that has collapsed or been destroyed

sandstone (SAND-stohn)—rock that includes sand and some cement

tribe (TRIBE)—a group of people who share the same language and way of life

Read More

Cunningham, Kevin, and Peter Benoit. *The Pueblo.* True Book. New York: Children's Press, 2011.

Jenson-Elliott, Cindy. *Desert Communities Past and Present.* Who Lived Here? North Mankato, Minn.: Capstone Press, 2014.

Moss, Jenny. *Look Inside a Pueblo.* Look Inside. Mankato, Minn.: Capstone Press, 2010.

Internet Sites

FactHound offers a safe, fun way to find Internet sites related to this book. All of the sites on FactHound have been researched by our staff.

Here's all you do:

Visit *www.facthound.com*

Type in this code: 9781491403150

Super-cool stuff! Check out projects, games and lots more at
www.capstonekids.com

Index

Critical Thinking Using the Common Core

1. What is a kiva? How was it used? What made it special? (Key Ideas and Details)

2. Look at the photo on page 17. What is happening in the photo? Could this area of the village be used for other events? Say what. (Integration of Knowledge and Ideas)